THE SECRETS OF OUTSOURCING

How to Find the Perfect Freelancer

M. MORGAN

The Secrets of Outsourcing

Legal Note: The author of this book has used her knowledge and efforts with the objective of collecting the information appeared in this publication. The information contained in this book has character purely educative; in this sense, if the reader wishes to apply some of the ideas exposed in this book it will be under his or her own responsibility. The author, in any case, is not held responsible for any direct or indirect damage derived from the use (or misuse) of this book. The information included in this publication is offered in good faith and believing to be exact at the moment of its publication, being subjected to any necessary modifications.

Cover Image: Geralt/pixabay.com

Table of Content

Chapter I: Introduction 4

Chapter II: What Is Outsourcing? 7

Chapter III: Why Outsource? 12

Chapter IV: How to Use Outsourcing 17

Chapter V: What Are the Benefits to Outsourcing? 19

Chapter VI: Outsourcing Nowadays 23

Chapter VII: To Outsource or Not to Outsource? 31

Chapter VIII: How to Look for Freelancers 40

Chapter IX: Outsourcing Destinations 61

Chapter X: Negotiating the Outsourcing Deal 63

Chapter XI: Paying for a Project 65

Chapter XII: The Survival Guide for Outsourcing Sites 69

Chapter XIII: Conclusion 86

ANNEX 91

Chapter I: Introduction

Outsourcing is a practice developed by businesses since the beginning of commerce and trade. In the last years, this practice has become more and more common in the online world. At the moment, online entrepreneurs can also use this common business strategy with a great deal of effect.

Of course, outsourcing is not supposed to be used in every single step of your business, but understanding how it works and how it can benefit a business, it is possible to make an educated decision about when to use an outsourcing provider.

Delegating a part of your business to strangers can cause you some sleepless nights.

This is especially the case when business owners show an obsessive habit to check over every little detail of their enterprise, as they want things perfect. As a result they end up heavily editing, programming, writing, and promoting their projects.

Sometimes you may come across people who turn in inferior work making you waste time and money.

Nevertheless, most of the time freelancers deliver (even some of them over-deliver) high quality work that will help you boost the reputation and benefits of your business.

Remember that no one is blessed with all knowledge and you may need help when it comes down to programming or translating.

This book will teach you how to avoid the lemons in a basket of apples and how to protect yourself from low-quality freelancers by analyzing your business' needs, knowing where to find an appropriate provider, and making the best from your outsourcing experience.

Chapter II: What Is Outsourcing?

Outsourcing is the fact of utilizing resources that are outside the direct control of the company to handle tasks that are relevant to the operation and success of the business.

In other words, it consists of hiring a provider to handle a specific function for a specific period of time and with guidelines that are agreeable to both parties. In some cases, the service may be granted limited powers to act in the stead of the client, if that is necessary to perform the contracted tasks.

Regarding the payment, on the contrary that it happens with the in-house staff, it is usually pegged per project instead of the number of hours the worker actually works.

The main function of outsourcing is to allow employees to focus on company operations that may be more detailed and directly related to the growth of the business or to temporarily hire the knowledge of a professional in a certain field who knows more about a certain task than the rest of the staff.

Companies have been outsourcing work for decades.

As early as the 1950's, when telephones became an item common in most households, established enterprises were contracting housewives who were looking for an extra income to do the job of receptionists or secretaries.

Nowadays, it is estimated that more than 200 million people around the world work from home for an outside employer. This figure has exploded with the development of Internet, as it allows faster and greater connectivity between employers and outsourcing providers.

You may think that your business is not big enough to outsource a part of it but there is always room for outsourcing, but sometimes you will face situations when you need extra help. For instance, let's say that you have focused your efforts on writing e-books. At one point, you may consider the possibility of hiring the services of a professional writer who knows more than you about a certain field or perhaps, you wish to translate your e-book to different languages or need some extra editing to look more professional.

An outsider can do all these tasks for a reasonable price (between $30 and $200).

In exchange, it will provide you with a more professional product that will meet customers' expectations and will boost your sales.

Chapter III: Why Outsource?

The main reason to outsource part of the work, in most cases, is time. There are only 24 hours in a day and we spend around 7 or 8 hours sleeping; 2 or 3 hours commuting; another 2 or 3 hours eating; around 2 hours getting ready (having baths, grooming rituals, etc.) and this leaves us with around 10 more hours to spare. All this without considering that sometimes we need time to socialize, which means that many days we will have around 6 or 7 hours to work and this is probably not enough time when we are talking about settling down an online business.

Besides, bear in mind that the world of Internet marketing is in constant evolution and that you will need a great deal of time and effort to keep in contact with the new trends and tricks in the business.

If you could have a few more hours to dedicate to your business, you will come out with new ideas and develop more moneymaking products or more effective strategies that would have catapulted your business to the next level. Maybe you also have some time to search new markets, which you could have exploited for more profit or find out new profitable niches.

Perhaps, you could also have some spare time to build a solid relationship with your clients. Or you could have spent that time with your family, playing with your kids and pets.

You could have done a load of things with the time you spent dealing with putting all the weight of your business on your own shoulders.

Let's face it, you will actually spend most of the day preparing orders, writing reports and articles, elaborating e-books, dealing with customers' services, develop marketing strategies, updating your entries in blogs and your content in websites, etc. Eventually, all these tasks could be overwhelming, as sometimes you forget that that you are but one man (or woman).

The second main reason to hire the services of an outsider is that you are actually losing money by trying to do all this by yourself. More often than not, online marketers tend to think that hiring an outsourcing provider is a little expensive and they rather things be done their way.

However, in many cases you will see yourself losing some money because of your insistence on doing things yourself.

In the online world opportunities are lost every second that you are forced to stay away from other necessities of your business. These opportunities could translate to more earnings for you, if only you had the chance to pursue them.

Chapter IV: How to Use Outsourcing

Many small businesses make use of outsourcing to help keep operational costs to a minimum. For example, hiring the services of a payroll expert to calculate applicable taxes during the tax revenue period, will save us from paying permanent staff all year round while hiring the service of a cleaning lady for two hours a day, will save us from hiring a part-time lady that will work for around five hours a day with the corresponding expenses in salary and taxes for the company.

Also, hiring staff for sporadic events, like the launching of a marketing campaign, will save us from hiring the permanent services of marketers and public relations personnel.

Outsourcing may be also be utilized as a means of launching a short-term sales campaign to pitch a new product to an existing customer base. In brief, there are very few tasks within a company that cannot be outsourced.

Chapter V: What Are the Benefits to Outsourcing?

Outsourcing is a good decision for small businesses that are just trying to get established, as every dollar counts. On many occasions, outsourcing could be cheaper than buying necessary equipment, hiring and training personnel.

For example, managing the finances or IT departments of a company will require hiring at least one paid professional who will not consider the position, at least you offer a decent salary and some benefits. By outsourcing these functions to an accounting or IT firm, the client will pay a monthly rate, much lower than a salary, and not have to be concerned about providing a benefits package. The savings in this one instance can be substantial.

For the online entrepreneur that wants to look like a "real" company, outsourcing tasks like answering the phone or customer care will give him/her more time for building the business and winning new clients.

The end result is a more aggressive sales and marketing effort while still maintaining a professional image.

By hiring someone, you would expand your business and become more competitive, as you will get rid of some of the workload and are able to produce more at a faster rate. All this will contribute to a boost of income, as you will have more time to dedicate to your customers.

Outsourcing will also help you to meet multiple deadlines, as by delegating work, you will be assured that the business activity will continue even when you are away.

By getting the services of an outside provider the quality of the products or services that you offer could increase, as you can take advance of the professional capabilities and knowledge of other people. Outsourcing will allow you to choose a freelancer whose field of expertise deals with a specific task, and this will result in the improvement of your business.

In brief, outsourcing will provide you with the required manpower when it is needed in order to adjust your business to the changing demands in the market.

Chapter VI: Outsourcing Nowadays

The development of Internet has created a global market of potential clients and international workforce. At the same time, the using of outsourcing providers has become a habitual practice in today's business world. Areas of business that are popularly outsourced include:

- Consultancy- Consultants are one of the first groups of freelancers in the history of the commercial world, as, at some point, all of us need the advice of an expert on a certain field. Popular areas where consultancy is sought include search engine optimization, financial planning, legal advice, or marketing.

- Customer Service- Customer care, including answering enquiries and shipping products, is one of the most time consuming tasks in any business and spending long hours developing an appropriate customer service could leave you without enough time to dedicate to the rest of your business.

- IT Support- Being a computer expert takes skills and years of training and experience. Bearing in mind that nowadays any business is heavily dependent on online resources for its existence, IT services are a must.

- Translation Projects- In a globalized world it is basically a must to translate your content into different languages in order to reach the major number of potential clients possible and to attract more traffic and visitors to your website or blog.

For example, if you have written an e-book you should consider the possibility of reaching a wider audience if you had it translated into a variety of languages.

Bearing in mind that you are selling a book, grammar mistakes are not allowed here and therefore, it is necessary to find a freelance translator that will be able to deliver high standard translations that will help you market your product and develop a good reputation.

It is highly recommended here to avoid the use of automatic online translators that are not able to properly translate expressions or slang and will find it highly difficult to differentiate between pronouns, verbs, and adjective agreements.

- Accounting- Lets' face it, not everyone has enough accountancy skills and time to take on board the bills, costs, payments, and profits generated by business, especially when the business grows and it involves staff.

- Data Entry/Encoding- Can you imagine how long you would have to spend on updating volumes of data? Ask yourself this question and consider if it is worth your time to hire an outsider to take care of the task.

- Web Design, Development, and Updating- Although there are a number of software programs and hosting that will allow you to build your own website in just a few hours, it takes skills to create a truly captivating and effective site while it takes a considerable amount of time to keep it updated.

- Graphic Design- Once again, there are plenty of software programs available in the market that will help you out when it comes down to developing an almost professional design and maybe this is the best option out there when you are just starting your business and do not have enough money to spend.

Nonetheless, these programs are not able to replace the talent of a good professional designer and grant you an eye-catching and exclusive design. Therefore, if you can afford to go for it, hire a professional designer to create the covers of your e-books, for instance. You will have original, exclusive, and professional covers that will call the attention of buyers (in the online world the cover represents 80% of the sale).

- Writing & Editing- If you want to create an e-book, articles, reports, posts, catching sales letters, or content and you do not have the talent or time to dedicate to this task, you need to find a ghostwriter who does the job for you.

- Secretarial Duties- Nowadays, you can have your own digital secretary that can fulfill a variety of tasks such as answering emails, attending phone calls, dealing with customers, etc. The best thing is that you can always assign almost any kind of work for your digital assistant without having to pay taxes and insurance as for an in-house member of the staff.

Chapter VII: To Outsource or Not to Outsource?

As everything in life outsourcing has many benefits ("borrow" specialized skills and knowledge from other professionals and saving time in certain tasks and money in equipment, personnel training, and staff taxes) and some disadvantages (loss of control over the operations outsourced and delegation of functions and decision making over the contractee).

Outsourcing is like hiring employees and you should bear in mind that sometimes you hire a very good professional but sporadically, that is not the case.

It is essential that you set a deadline to deliver the project and specific guidelines or, in case, you will see yourself having to polish and finish the project. It is also crucial that you find another person to do the job if your outsourcing service does not fulfill with the agreement, as failure to take corrective actions could lead to financial losses.

Making the decision of outsourcing some functions is a tough one. At the end of the day, you are taking decisions over your workforce, your financial situation, and whether or not the jobs being outsourced are important enough to keep nearby.

When it comes to outsourcing, you should ask yourself some very important questions.

1. Will outsourcing hinder or help my business? You have to know beforehand that outsourcing is not for everyone. For instance, if you are taking the first steps with your business, a financial investment is out of your reach, as no one will work for free and most freelancers require preliminary payment before taking your project on board.

2. What do you expect to get out of the outsourcing: time, knowledge that you do not have, or avoiding hiring additional staff? Knowing what you want from outsourcing will help you decide whether or not to hire an outsider.

3. How much can you pay for outsourcing services? It is essentially finding the balance between what you have and what you need.

If you do not have enough money to outsource all the tasks that you wished, you have to decide which one will provide the most benefit currently.

4. How long will the outsourcing project last?- It is a short project or will it be going on for an indefinite period of time? Many outsourcing service providers offer discounts if you use their services for a few years, which could mean an attractive discount.

Make sure there are terms and conditions in the contract that give you a "way out" if they fail to deliver services as outlined in the agreement.

5. Is my business one that has portions that could be easily outsourced? You will need to analysis the structure of your business and determine whether or not some areas should and can be outsourced, bearing in mind that some divisions can be more easily outsourced than others.

6. Finally, do some research on the companies or freelance professionals that you intend to hire for your outsourcing.

Are they reputable? Can they provide you with the service that you and your customers deserve? Are they charging a fair rate? Can they actually do the job adequately?

When outsourcing a task you should develop a project description that unites everything that you expect from a project and a guideline that the freelancer has to strictly follow. In doing so, you have to write down what you wish to have done and what is the purpose of the project. You will also need to specify how the project should achieve its purpose and what is your target audience and how the project can meet their needs. Finally, decide how the freelancer should approach the project and how it should be marketed.

At the moment of outsourcing you should:

I. Determine the goals of your business.

II. Determine if outsourcing will help you meet those goals.

III. Know the areas that you can outsource.

IV. Find a competent freelancer and reach a reasonable deal according price.

V. Check up on the status of the project from time to time.

VI. Check if deliverables meet your expectations and require corrections if necessary.

VII. Payment and close the deal.

The best idea is to take care of every aspect of your business as much as you can, but when this interferes in your growth or it is mining your reputation, then the moment has arrived to outsource some tasks to professionals who could grant you the time or knowledge that you are lacking of.

Remember that a freelancer is an expert in a certain field and he or she can actually suggest proposals that you have not previously thought about.

Chapter VIII: How to Look for Freelancers

Once you have decided that outsourcing is a viable option for your business, it is time to look for the right person to deliver the job. Choosing the wrong person can result in a considerable waste of money, time, and energy, as you may end up doing the work yourself while running out of time. Therefore, it is essential to choose the right person although it means that, at least during the first few projects, you will have to show a great deal of trust.

Outsourcing does not mean that you are going to take a portion of your business to another country, but simply means that you are handing a portion of your work to another business.

There are a number of steps that you should follow in order to find the most efficient and trustworthy provider possible:

1. **Determinate the Job You Wish to Delegate**

The first step to leave clear before hiring the services of an outsider is to determine what area/s of your business needs to be outsourced.

In general, it should be something that you cannot do for yourself or something that you do not have the time for. It is crucial to develop a basic criterion of what you need, how you need it done, and what deadline to set.

2. Where to Find a Freelancer

The Internet is a big place where you can get lost if you are not careful but where you can also find a qualified freelancer for any tasks that you wish to outsource. There are a number of places where you could find an appropriate freelancer to outsource some of the areas of your business.

Although you always can use traditional methods like placing an advertisement on a local newspaper, the best place to find freelancers is online, as users are always looking for earning opportunities and you will have access to a large worldwide database of possible providers.

Some interesting places to have a look are:

- Auction Sites- These are websites where you can place your project proposal and freelancers can bid on it.

    You can choose the lowest bidder, or otherwise, the most qualified one whom you think would turn in the highest quality of work possible; it all depends on your purpose and your budget.

The best auction sites for freelancers are: www.rentacoder.com, www.scriptance.com, www.elance.com and www.fiverr.com.

- College Students- Students can turn into specialized and qualified freelancers willing to earn some extra cash. As they have yet to acquire their degrees (and therefore they are not professionals), you could acquire their services for reasonable rates.

Basically, every college or university has community sites where you can contact your future freelancer or post a message with your offer.

- Editorial Guilds- These are communities of writers and editors who are looking for extra work.

Sometimes you will not have to pay for their services as long as you display their work on your site and they could use it as part of the portfolio they are building to increase their reputation as writers.

- Forums and Social Networking Platforms- Most specialized forums and social networking sites like Facebook, LinkedIn, or Twitter have a classified ads section where service providers can advertise themselves. Also, some forums have a job section where you can have access to qualified freelancers.

3.- Choosing the Perfect Freelancer

The key to outsourcing a project is to find that efficient provider who will turn in quality work for a reasonable price while avoiding those others who fail to deliver our expectations of the project.

The next step is to build a list that includes the skills that the future outsourcing agent must have to fulfill every task, bearing in mind that he or she must accommodate your needs and not the other way around. Otherwise, the main reason to hire outsourcing (saving yourself time and headaches) will disappear.

One of the most important characteristics of a freelancer is the ability to consistently meet deadlines or you will lose customers and waste time having to constantly contact the outsourcing agent to check whether or not your task is ready. The idea behind outsourcing tasks is to make life easier, not create extra complications.

You need an outsourcing service provider who can make decisions, especially when it comes down to outsourcing the PR of the company or the organization of an event or marketing campaign. When the provider is unable to deal with the situation, you could end up losing business and mining your reputation.

Consequently, at the moment of hiring an outsourcing agent who must be able to accomplish decision-making, interview him/her carefully, presenting the person with different hypothetical scenarios, the answers of the expert will give you an idea about how that person will react under stressful situations.

Try to avoid problematic characters and if a provider has given you headaches in the past, avoid hiring his/her services again. Take the task seriously and remember that although the outsourcing provider is doing the job, the results will reflect on you.

When hiring an outsourcing provider ask yourself whether or not that contractee will do the work as well as your in-house staff and require references and samples of previous works.

Before you hire the service of a freelancer, there are a series of questions that you should address to avoid unpleasant surprises:

- Make sure that the freelancer understands every single detail involved in the project and encourage him/her to ask questions.

Keep communications open until the end of the project, as a lack of communication or misunderstanding could end in the freelancer submitting work completely different than what you expected.

- Check qualifications and References- Especially when it comes down to large and expensive projects as, sadly, a common problem is that the freelancer is not as qualified as he/she claimed.

The good news is that auction sites usually have checks against false claims while other sites will leave you susceptible to them.

- Demand Exclusive Rights When Necessary- If you hire the services of an outside provider to build an exclusive product for you, make sure that you keep full rights for it upon delivery by asking the freelancer to sign an exclusive rights agreement.

In this case, if later on you discover that the freelancer sold the same product to another client, you could claim your rights legally.

Do not worry, most times things do not go to that extent, as when a freelancer signs the agreement he or she knows that he/she is committing a legal crime if they decide to violate the contract.

- Require a Confidentiality Agreement- When you hire the services of a ghostwriter, designer, or any creative professional, ask the person to sign a confidential contract that includes a formal renounce to any copyrights over the project. In this way, you are paying for the project to make it yours and to sign as the author and get all the royalties from it.

Sadly, there have been cases in which the people have required the services of a ghostwriter to write a book and after putting a lot of money and effort into promoting the book in question, the ghostwriter has legally claimed the rights to royalties, as he or she never renounced to the copyrights. So, make sure that this is the case upon complexion of the project.

- Do Not Pay in Advance- Never pay the totality of the price upfront, at least when you are using a auction site it grants you some protection in case the freelancer fails to deliver or sends you a completely different project, otherwise you are taking the risk of losing time and money.

To make sure that you hire the right person, you should also consider some general advices like checking the age of the provider (a person too young could be unprofessional, although it is not always the case plus a contract with someone underage is not bidding); know the nationality of the freelancer (especially when you need a translation); check the educational background of the provider and get a real expert, avoiding those who pretend to be an expert but wish to make your project their training opportunity (some auction sites give you the chance of verifying qualifications); study the freelancer's portfolio (request previous samples and references); and choose a freelancer that is willing to bend for your schedule, not the other way around.

If you want to use channels other than freelancers' sites, you can request documentation that will prove the identities and qualifications.

At the end of the day, you are paying and it is your right as a consumer, so exercise it.

4.- Protecting Yourself

By delegating your project to an outside service provider you lose control over the creation process. It is vital that you protect your business interests against any eventuality.

If you hire the services of a freelancer through an outsourcing site, every winning bid will be considered a binding contract between you and the freelancer. Besides, you will be entitled to use an arbitration service in case of disagreements between the parts. This will assure you of an objective party who will mediate discussions on the non-observance of certain terms and conditions.

However, if you want to hire a freelancer outside these platforms, you will be on your own.

On the other hand, the best freelancers are actually found outside the auction platforms, as highly qualified professionals are not willing to grant their services through bids and require a higher payment than the ones offered on those sites and they do not have to pay a commission (around 15%) to the outsourcing websites for finding the clients.

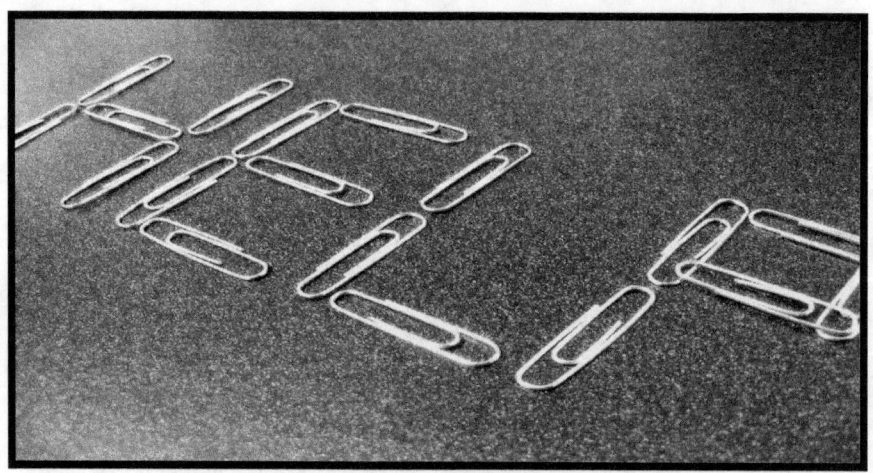

In brief, highly qualified freelancers would rather promote their services through the strength of the reputation they have built for themselves and would rather do their own marketing instead of relying on clients provided by outsourcing sites.

Also, you might end up paying less, as some quality work will be placed at high amounts to cover the site's applicable fees.

Choosing between outsourcing sites and dealing directly with the freelancer can be quite a dilemma, as each has its advantages and disadvantages.

If you choose to deal with the freelancer directly, the best thing to do here is to require the freelancer of your election to sign a contract. But make sure that the original signatures are stamped on the contract.

This means that you should ask the freelancer to send the agreement through fax or mail a signed copy, or scan a copy and email it.

In the last years, a name typed at the end of the contract; a digital signature; a unique password, code, or personal identification number; or a digital signature created through the use of encryption technology are also consider legally binding signatures.

At the end of this book, you can find templates of a work for hire contract and a non-disclosure agreement. Feel free to print and use them.

5.- Start Small

The first time that you hire a freelancer, try to breakdown your work into smaller parts to minimize losses in case the provider fails to deliver.

If you give the freelancer a large project, you will have to pay for the totality of the work even if the delivered project is not what you expected.

Chapter IX: Outsourcing Destinations

When deciding to go with a freelancer, you should bear in mind the nationality of your prospective temporary employee to facilitate communications and to guarantee a solid educative background that will give your project a professional touch.

Usually, freelancers from the United States, Canada, and Western European countries can offer a highly professional service and save your business around 8 to 17% of the normal operating costs, on the average.

The cost of living in a certain country is also a factor to bear in mind at the moment of determining the price of a freelancer.

For instance, freelancers from western countries might not be able to compete with freelancers based on countries like India or the Philippines, as the cost of living in the western hemisphere is significantly higher and, therefore, the rate per hour for a western provider is more elevated.

In fact, a business could save more than 1,000% in projects by hiring people in countries with a lower cost of living and that is the reason why they have become so popular.

However, bear in mind that a lower cost of living also means a lower level of general education in most cases with India and the Philippines being, in general terms, the exception.

Chapter X: Negotiating the Outsourcing Deal

When negotiating a service with an outsourcing provider, many companies will offer you their services at a flat rate but sometimes there is some room for negotiation. The most important thing to consider is to carefully read throughout the contract and conditions of your future provider (hiring the services of a lawyer if necessary), reviewing all of the materials sent to you by the outsourcing business. At this time, you should consider taking a trip to the outsourcing business to see the level of professionalism and working atmosphere while checking out their products and the options they offer.

Try to negotiate for a trial period where you will pay the company for short period of time at an agreed to price. If the outsourcing company does not offer a trial period, consider hiring another provider instead. If the trial period is satisfactory, you can sign the contract.

When you do not have enough experience writing an appropriate business contract or you are planning to outsource to a foreign country, the best advice is to hire the services of a middle-man, as a third party outsourcing agency will contact the necessary people to help determine how to draft an international contract and hire people abroad.

Chapter XI: Paying for a Project

The main rule when it comes down to payment is to always haggle for a lower price.

Bear in mind that a freelancer could be flexible about rates and usually his or her projects come out with a suggested retail price. Therefore, you should learn to negotiate for the lowest price.

These are some tips that will help you obtain the best price possible out of a provider:

- Offer a long-term deal leaving clear that if you are happy with the results, more projects will come in the future. Having more earnings in the future, will push the freelancer towards offering you a lower price.

- State your budget clearly to avoid an increment of price in the future. Also state that you have had offers at that price but do not offer a miserable price and be reasonable or you will end up with very low quality work, as any good professional and qualified freelancer will find it insulting.

After setting the price, you should agree the payment method. You could pay the full price upon delivery when you check the final state of the product (usually freelancers do not accept this type of payment although there are exceptions); paying 50% of the price upon acceptance of the project and the other 50% upon satisfactory delivery of the final product (the most common); or paying 1/3 of the total upon acceptance of the project, another 1/3 midway or after partial delivery and the final 1/3 upon satisfactory delivery of the final product.

Whatever you do, do not pay the total amount before the project is delivered and you are happy with the results; at least if you hire work through a website your are protected in the case that the freelancer hands you a poor quality project or sometimes does not meet your expectations at all.

Chapter XII: The Survival Guide for Outsourcing Sites

The outsourcing platforms work in a similar way to eBay. You basically have to post your project and set a specific deadline for delivery and the freelancers will bid on it.

Then, you have the option of choosing among the different freelancers. You can get the cheapest or the most qualified.

The best piece of advice here is to check the freelancers' qualifications, previous works, and references.

Rentacoder.com

This site, www.rentacoder.com, is one of the most popular sites for freelancers, literally reuniting thousands of professionals from around the world.

You will have to set up a free account and then log in (at the bottom of the site) every time you want to enter the site.

The next step is to visit the section "Buyers" where you could post a bid by clicking on "My Bid Requests". At this point, you will be redirected to another screen.

Posting a bid is free and you can do so by clicking on "Request Bids".

You are not obligated to choose any bid that you receive if you are not totally sure about it, but a non-action on a project you offer will be displayed on your Buyer Score that, although it is not that important, you will like to maintain a clean record just in case.

You will be required to introduce your email address, password, and username.

Then, click on "Open Auction" as you still do not know the freelancers yet. In the future, when you know a certain freelancer and you want to hire his/her services in particular, you can choose other auction types.

On the next screen, you will be required to introduce a description of your project. Be as specific and clear as possible.

Then, you will need to enter the platform where your project will be used, to verify that the format in which the project is delivered is readable by the operating system.

At this point you will have to click on the "Next" bottom and enter a specific deadline and budget for your project or choose the option "open for fair suggestions." You can also specify the duration of the bidding process.

Finally, you will be required to verify the details you have provided and return to the home page where you can visit the section "My Buyer Financials" where you can control the bids received on your project.

The platform also offers the possibility of sending an email every time that someone places a bid.

Accepting a Bid

Accepting a bid is easy, as your control panel will grant you access to the details of the bids but you must do whatever it takes to make sure that you are choosing the right person. By clicking on the bidder's username, you will be directed to a page where you can find a resume, portfolio, and history of the freelancer within the site, as well as, reviews on his/her previous works. These reviews are opinions of previous customers, which should be detailed, check to find clues about the professionalism of the freelancer that you are about to hire.

Besides the reviews, it is also essential to check the score of the freelancers, which appears alongside his/her username, as it reflects the degree of satisfaction of buyers who have hired his/her services before. But, be careful, as the newcomers do not have scores and that does not mean that they cannot be qualified and experts.

Do not commit the most common of the mistakes of expecting high quality when choosing a really low price and remember that, in general, you get what you pay for. However, there will be times when your expectations will be more than met.

You can communicate with the bidders through private messages, they will have the chance to ask questions.

When you choose a freelancer, just click on "View or Accept".

Paying

You can pay for your bid using PayPal or credit card and the payment is placed under escrow. This means that you will have the chance of receiving a refund in case the freelancer fails to deliver.

Once your payment has been placed under escrow, the freelancer will start on your project.

Communication is essential to make sure that the project goes on according to your expectations. It is highly recommended to use the site's messaging system so you will have reference in the event the freelancer fails to deliver and you require a refund. These messages will be the best proof in case of arbitration due to disagreements.

If the work entails an amount higher than $150, rentacoder.com requires the freelancer to report the progress of the project once a week. You can require the freelancer to let you know about the state of your project more often or if you project cost less than $150.

The freelancer will let you know when the order is ready through an email and your project will be stored in the server of rentacoder.com to be downloaded.

If the delivery covers your expectations, you can authorize the release of the payment held in escrow. In case you are not satisfied you can ask the freelancer for some corrections or revisions. You will be asked to rate the freelancer. If you are satisfied, it is recommended to give a rate between 8 and 10.

In the event of disagreement, you can resolve the dispute through the arbitration system of rentacoder.com.

Then, it will be your chance of reporting your communication recorded in the messaging system.

Elance.com

This outsourcing site, www.elance.com, works very similarly to www.rentacoder.com but the difference is that freelancers can choose between opening a free account or paying a membership to have access to potential clients.

As a client, elance.com grants you access to freelancers' qualifications, portfolio, and academic background and professionalism of those members on the paid area. This will guarantee you good service.

Nevertheless, some of them will go very high when bidding for a project, as they have to pay a percent of it to the site. You will have the option to open your project for members with free accounts whose history is not verifiable but they offer lower bids.

More often than not you will discover that membership accounts are not necessarily the highest quality and free accounts does not mean bad quality.

There are occasional surprises of very low bids from new providers delivering outstanding work.

Setting up an account and bidding for a project follows a similar process as on www.rentacoder.com.

Pros

1. This site attracts more highly qualified freelancers.

2. Elance.com guarantees the reliability and professionalism of freelancers in exchange for a reasonable charge.

3. Elance.com is a better choice for smaller projects; always go for free account freelancers because on www.rentacoder.com freelancers usually do not bid for small projects, as they will have to give 15% to the site.

Cons

1. You will get higher bids compared to www.rentacoder.com. You will be charged $25 if you choose a paid freelancer to be deposited in advanced and paid by credit card.

2. Elance.com only offers their arbitration system for buyers who choose a paid member. This means that you are basically unprotected in case of disagreement.

As on other sites, enter a clear specification and deadline for your project; keep communications going with the freelancer, check his/her educational background and previous works (requiring samples and/or references and reading the reviews left by other buyers); make sure that the freelancer has enough experience; be wary of awarding big projects to untested freelancers; require the freelancers to sign a non-disclosure agreement through which he refuses any future claim on copyrights; negotiate after-delivery support in case of technical projects; make sure that the payment scheme is clearly defined; put everything in writing through the message service provided by the website to make sure that you have proof in case of requiring the arbitration process.

Scriptlance.com

Scriptlance.com is an outsourcing site that offers very good deals.

Pros

1. Transactions are easy to process. Once you set up an account, you just have to deposit a minimum of $5 and make sure that your account is never on 0 or it will be frozen.

2. You will be charged $5 for each project, which is cheaper than Elance.com.

3. You can use the same account to offer a project and to bid for a project offered by other buyers. So, you can be a buyer and freelancer with the same account.

4. Payment transactions are free of charge.

Cons

1. Buyers are not protected against disagreements.

2. There is not a score system but you can check profiles and previous buyers' reviews through the message boards that can also be used to communicate with freelancers.

3. There are not as many freelancers as on Elance.com or Rentcoder.com.

In general, most Internet marketers agree on the fact that Rentacoder.com is the best choice thanks to its buyer protection system, its arbitration resort, and its large database of freelancers. However, bear in mind that you will also have to deal with a higher number of under-qualified freelancers who will bid for your projects.

Chapter XIII: Conclusion

After collecting all the necessary information regarding outsourcing, now it is the time to ask yourself: should or should I not outsource some of the tasks of my business? This is a question that only you can answer because every business is built in a different way.

If you want to have total control over your enterprise, then outsourcing is not for you, as you might end up redoing the work that you paid for. But if you want to make the best out of your time while boosting your profit, then you should seriously consider delegating some tasks to freelancers. Outsourcing not only guarantees us more spare time to dedicate to our businesses but also to our social lives.

Besides, it does not matter how intelligent, efficient, and educated you are, as no human being knows everything about anything and therefore, sooner or later, you will come across a task that will make you feel hopeless and lacking of the necessary knowledge, the skills that a particular freelancer may have and which you can "borrow" by outsourcing that task.

The key of outsourcing lays in the fact of knowing your business indefinitely and analyzing which part or parts of it could be outsourced. Then the next crucial step is to make sure that you choose the right person for the job.

In brief, outsourcing can be one of the best moves you will ever make for your business. Just analyze what you need, take the time to find the right freelancer for the job, and establish a strong working relationship with him/her. Once you accomplish this, you can focus your efforts on making your company stronger and more profitable, which would not have been possible otherwise.

Just remember to protect yourself and your business' interests, as the purpose of outsourcing is to make your business more efficient and not the other way around.

After reading this book, you will have an idea of how to analyze the needs of your business and where to find an efficient freelancer that will help you out at the moment of outsourcing some tasks. Now, it is entirely up to you to take the next step and start to boost benefits. Remember that you do not hold all of the knowledge in the world and that any business is in need of some investment to really take off.

Take the first small step in the world of outsourcing, learn and grow wise and soon you will be realizing that investing a small fraction of your money in outsourcing will pay off, granting to your business more profits (and reputation) that you could ever imagine.

ANNEX

TEMPLATE 1: WORK FOR HIRE CONTRACT

AN AGREEMENT

This agreement, executed by _____ whose contact details appear below and shall be referred to herein as the EMPLOYER for brevity, and _____ whose contact details also appear below and shall be referred to herein as the EMPLOYEE, hereby witness that:

1. The Employee binds himself to perform work for the Employer on a project with the following specifications:

(Enter the details of the project here. Include deadline for submission and all matters the freelancer should agree to.)

2. The Employer binds himself to pay the Employee for the work done, once it is satisfactorily delivered, in the total amount of _____

3. Payment shall be made in three parts. 1/3 of the stipulated amount shall be paid to the Employee upon acceptance of the project. 1/3 shall be paid midway through the project. The remaining 1/3 shall be paid upon final and satisfactory delivery of the project. (Payment scheme can be different from this. It could be 50/50, or 100% upon final delivery. Simply adjust this provision correspondingly.)

4. The Employee binds himself to complete the work to the best of his abilities, to always strive for the highest possible quality with regards to every aspect of the project, and to deliver an original and unique product in compliance with the specifications of the project.

5. The Employee binds himself to transmit all rights to the product to the Employer upon delivery of the product. The Employee cannot retract this designation of rights. The transmittal of rights shall be final and irrevocable.

6. The Employee binds himself to assume full legal responsibilities as well as an obligation to indemnify the Employer in the event that what he has delivered would be found to be unoriginal, stolen, plagiarized, or otherwise illegal.

7. The Employee binds himself to reimburse the Employer for what the latter has paid in the event that the project will not be completed because of a reason that is not attributable to the Employer.

8. The Employer and the Employee shall be granted the power to rescind this agreement in the event that the other party violates, wittingly or unwittingly, the terms of this document.

9. This agreement shall be deemed as completed upon satisfactory delivery by the Employee and upon full payment by the Employer.

In witness whereof, both parties give their assent to this agreement this _____ day of _____, 20--.

_____

EMPLOYER

(Contact details)

_____

EMPLOYEE

(Contact details)

TEMPLATE 2: NON-DISCLOSURE AGREEMENT

THIS AGREEMENT governs the disclosure of information by and between Alpha and Beta as of _____(the "Effective Date").

1. Definition of Confidential Information

As used herein, "Confidential Information" shall mean any and all technical and non-technical information related to _____ provided by either party to the other, including but not limited to (a) patent(s) and patent applications, (b) trade secret, and (c) copyrighted information (d) proprietary information-- ideas, techniques, sketches, drawings, works of authorship, models, inventions, know-how, processes, apparatuses, equipment, algorithms, software programs, software source documents, and formulae related to the current, future, and proposed products and services of each of the parties.

This includes, without limitation, their respective information concerning research, experimental work, development, design details and specifications, engineering, financial information, procurement requirements, purchasing, manufacturing, customer lists, investors, employees, business and contractual relationships, business forecasts, sales and merchandising, marketing plans, and information the disclosing party provides regarding third parties.

2. Identification of Confidential Information

If the Confidential Information is embodied in tangible material (including without limitation, software, hardware, drawings, graphs, charts, disks, tapes, prototypes, and samples), it shall be labeled as "Confidential" or bear a similar legend. If the Confidential Information is disclosed orally or visually, it shall be identified as such at the time of disclosure.

3. Exceptions to Confidential Information

Each party's obligations under this Agreement with respect to any portion of the other party's Confidential Information shall terminate when the party to whom Confidential Information was disclosed (the "Recipient") can document that: (a) it was in the public domain at the time it was communicated to the Recipient by the other party; (b) it entered the public domain subsequent to the time it was communicated to the Recipient by the other party through no fault of the Recipient; (c) it was in the Recipient's possession free of any obligation of confidence at the time it was communicated to the Recipient by the other party; (d) it was rightfully communicated to the Recipient free of any obligation of confidence subsequent to the time it was communicated to the Recipient by the other party; (e) it was developed by employees or agents of the Recipient independently of and without reference to any information communicated to the Recipient by the other party;

(f) the communication was in response to a valid order by a court or other governmental body, was otherwise required by law, or was necessary to establish the rights of either party under this Agreement or (g) it was not identified as Confidential Information of the disclosing party in accordance with Section 2.

4. Handling of Confidential Information

Each party agrees that at all times and notwithstanding any termination or expiration of this Agreement it will hold in strict confidence and not disclose to any third party Confidential Information of the other, except as approved in writing by the other party to this Agreement, and will use the Confidential Information for no purpose other than_____ with the other party to this Agreement. Each party shall only permit access to Confidential

Information of the other party to those of its employees or authorized representatives having a need to know and who have signed confidentiality agreements or are otherwise bound by confidentiality obligations at least as restrictive as those contained herein.

5. Confidentiality Agreement Residual Knowledge

Recipient may use its knowledge retained in intangible form in the unaided memories of its directors, employees, contractors and advisors as a result of exposure to the disclosing party's ("Discloser") Confidential Information. The Discloser acknowledges that the Recipient may have in conception or development technology and/or software which may be very similar or even identical to Discloser's Confidential Information and, as long as the Recipient obides by Section 4 herein, Discloser shall have no rights in such technology and/or software.

6. Agreement Term and Termination

This Agreement shall terminate two (2) year(s) after the Effective Date. The Recipient's obligations under this Agreement shall survive termination of the Agreement between the parties and shall be binding upon the Recipient's heirs, successors and assigns for a period of five (5) years.

Upon written request of the other party, a party shall promptly return to the other all documents and other tangible materials representing the other's Confidential Information and all copies thereof.

7. Confidentiality Agreement Warranties

Each party represents and warrants to the other party that (i) it has the requisite corporate authority to enter into and perform this Agreement, and (ii) its execution and performance under this Agreement, including its disclosure of Confidential Information to the Recipient, will not result in a breach of any obligation to any third party or infringe or otherwise violate any third party's rights.

8. No Export

Neither party shall export, directly or indirectly, any technical data acquired from the other pursuant to this Agreement or any product utilizing any such data to any country for which the U.S. Government or any agency thereof at the time of export requires an export license or other governmental approval without first obtaining such license or approval.

9. No Reverse Engineering

Each of the parties agrees that the software programs of the other party contain valuable confidential information and each party agrees it will not modify, reverse engineer, decompile, create other works from, or disassemble any software programs contained in the Confidential Information of the other party without the prior written consent of the other party.

10. No Grant of Rights

The parties recognize and agree that nothing contained in this Agreement shall be construed as granting any property rights, by license or otherwise, to any Confidential Information of the other party disclosed pursuant to this Agreement, or to any invention or any patent, copyright, trademark, or other intellectual property right that has issued or that may issue, based on such Confidential Information.

11. Equitable Remedies

Recipient acknowledges that Recipient's breach of this Agreement may cause irreparable harm to Discloser for which Discloser is entitled to seek injunctive or other equitable relief as well as monetary damages.

12. Confidentiality Agreement Miscellaneous

Neither party shall not transfer or assign this Agreement to any other person or entity, whether by operation of law or otherwise, without the prior written consent of the other. Any such attempted assignment shall be void and of no effect.

This Agreement shall be governed by, enforced under, and construed and interpreted in accordance with, the laws of California without reference to conflict of laws principles. Each party agrees consents to venue and personal jurisdiction in XXX.

If any provision of this Agreement is found by a proper authority to be unenforceable or invalid such unenforceability or invalidity shall not render this Agreement unenforceable or invalid as a whole and in such event, such provision shall be changed and interpreted so as to best accomplish the objectives of such unenforceable or invalid provision within the limits of applicable law.

Neither party will assign or transfer any rights or obligations under this Agreement, including by operation of law, without the prior written consent of the other party.

The Agreement is the complete and exclusive agreement regarding the disclosure of Confidential Information between the parties, and replaces any prior oral or written communications between the parties regarding Confidential Information. This Agreement may be signed in multiple copies, each of which shall constitute the same instrument.

Once completely executed, any reproduction of this Agreement made by reliable means shall be considered an original.

IN WITNESS WHEREOF, the parties hereto have caused this Confidentiality Agreement to be executed as of the Effective Date.

EMPLOYER

(Contact details)

_____

EMPLOYEE

(Contact details)

Illustrations

1. Too Much Work. Author: Pam & Phil/ www.flickr.com
2. Enterpreneur's Mind. Author: thetaxhaven on www.flickr.com
3. Free Time. Author: thetaxhaven/ www.flickr.com
4. Networking. Author: thetaxhaven/ www.flickr.com
5. Business. Author: thetaxhaven/ www.flickr.com
6. Writing & Editing. Author: thetaxhaven/ www.flickr.com
7. Customer Skills. Author: Bill Branson (Photographer) on www.commons.wikipedia.org.
8. Success. Author: thetaxhaven/ www.flickr.com
9. Tasks. Author: plantoo47 www.flickr.com
10. Do To List. Author: thetaxhaven/ www.flickr.com
11. Help. Author: banspy/ www.flickr.com
12. Becoming Rich. Author: thetaxhaven/ www.flickr.com
13. Meeting. Author: thetaxhaven/www.flickr.com

www.ingramcontent.com/pod-product-compliance
Lightning Source LLC
Chambersburg PA
CBHW051729170526
45167CB00002B/859